The Battle for the Mind

The Battle for the Mind

Jessie Penn-Lewis

Fort Washington, PA 19034

The Battle for the Mind
Published by CLC Publications

U.S.A.
P.O. Box 1449, Fort Washington, PA 19034

UNITED KINGDOM
CLC International (UK)
51 The Dean, Alresford, Hampshire, SO24 9BJ

Originally published by
The Overcomer Literature Trust
England

Printed in the United States of America
This printing 2015

ISBN (vital series): 978-0-87508-527-2
ISBN (e-book): 978-1-61958-048-0

Unless otherwise noted, Scripture quotations are from the Holy Bible, *King James Version*.

Scripture quotations marked CH are from *The Life and Epistles of St. Paul*, a translation and notes by W.J. Conybeare and J.S. Howson, 1851.

Italics in Scripture quotations are the emphasis of the author.

The Battle for the Mind

"I fear, lest by any means, as the serpent beguiled Eve through his subtilty, so your minds should be corrupted from the simplicity that is in Christ" (2 Corinthians 11:3).

There is a great battle today over the use and control of the mind, not only in the world but among the children of God. The apostle Paul, writing in 2 Corinthians 10:3–5, says: "For though living in the flesh, my warfare is not waged according to the flesh. For the weapons which I wield are not of fleshly weakness but mighty in the strength of God to overthrow the strongholds of the adversaries. Thereby can I *overthrow the reasonings* of the disputer and *pull down all lofty bulwarks* that raise themselves against the knowledge of God, and bring every *rebellious thought* into captivity and subjection to Christ" (*Conybeare*). In this passage we make the following observations:

1. The fact of a "war" declared by Paul.

First note the fact that the apostle declares that there is a "war" in which he is engaged. "My warfare," he says, "is not waged according to the flesh." This is in accord with his statements in other parts of his writings, notably Ephesians 6:10–18 and in his letters to Timothy (see 1 Tim. 1:18; 6:12; 2 Tim. 2:4; 4:7).

2. The battle for the mind described.

We see there is an aspect of the war described in this passage which has to do with the *mind*. "Thereby can I overthrow the *reasonings* of the disputer." In verse 4 (KJV) we read of a *"pulling down* of strongholds." The apostle seems to suggest that the mind is a "stronghold" which has to be pulled down, and every rebel thought in it made captive. A "stronghold" is generally held by an *enemy*, and truly there is an enemy holding the stronghold of the mind, according to 2 Corinthians 4:4, where it says that the "god of this world [age]" has "blinded the *minds* of them which believe not."

3. The condition of the mind by nature.

In various parts of the Pauline epistles we can identify very clearly the state of mind when held by the enemy as a stronghold. It is described in some cases as a "*reprobate mind*" (Rom. 1:28), a *blinded mind* (see 2 Cor. 3:14), a *darkened mind*, causing men to walk in the "*vanity of their minds*" (Eph. 4:17–19), intruding into things which the mind cannot fathom, "vainly puffed up" by a "*fleshly mind*" (Col. 2:18).

In Romans 8:7, the apostle says, "The *carnal mind* is enmity against God, for it is not subject to the law of God, neither indeed can be." This is confirmed in Colossians 1:21, where those who are unregenerated are described as "enemies" in the "*mind*;" and therefore alienated from God. We therefore clearly see how, in the natural man, the mind is "darkened," "puffed up" by the flesh, empty and vain in its thoughts, carnal because governed by the flesh, and in all its activities—whether apparently "good" or visibly "bad"—at enmity with God.

4. The unregenerate mind the stronghold of Satan.

The stronghold of the mind of man is therefore the strategic center of the "war" with the "god of this age," because it is primarily *through the mind* that he holds his captives in his power, and *through the mind* of those captives transmits (1) his poison into the minds of others, and (2) his plans and schemes for arousing those souls to active rebellion against God.

The mind of the Christian is also the strategic center of the "war on the saints" which Satan wages with ceaseless and fiendish skill. And for this reason: *the mind is the vehicle for the Spirit of God*, dwelling in the spirit of the believer, to transmit to others the truth of God, which alone can remove the deceptions of Satan which fill the minds of all who are in the darkness of nature. If the Holy Spirit is dwelling in the regenerate spirit have you considered the question of His *outlet*? If it were only by speech you would be an oracle! But there are no "oracles" on earth now. *The "oracles of God" are the Scriptures*. The Word of God is being displaced not only by the higher critics, but by many of God's own people by their taking supernatural "revelations" as being of equal authority with the written Scriptures. There are lives wrecked because they have turned from the Word of God to what they call direct revelation. There *is* a direct revelation by God the Holy Spirit illuminating the Word of God, and putting it into the spirit, but *not apart from* the Scriptures.

5. *The Holy Spirit and the mind of the believer.*

If *the mind is the vehicle of the Spirit* it is absolutely necessary that the Spirit of God should have full possession of it, with every "rebellious thought" brought into captivity to Christ. The Holy Spirit, dwelling in the spirit, needs the mind as a channel for expression, but it may be so blocked up and filled with other things that He is unable to transmit all He desires to do. A "blocked" mind means the spirit unexpressed, and a spirit unexpressed is a stoppage of the outflow of the Spirit of God to others.

6. *The mind of the Christian not fully delivered.*

This explains why numbers of God's children are unable to hold the truth of God which they hear, or to apply it to their lives, or express it to others. The mind *has never been fully delivered from the grip of the enemy*. Shall I put it crudely, and say that many get new "hearts" but they keep their old "heads"! They do not realize that unless the hold of the adversary, which he has through the fallen nature of man, is removed from the mind, he has a position of vantage in the life of the believer, *for attack and for hindrance in active service*. How many there are who have minds that never "think a thing out." Devoted children of God, with hearts full of love, but minds full of all kinds of mixture—minds that have not been renewed and delivered from the interference of the enemy. Consequently they have a strange lack of spiritual perception. They may get "flashes of light," and follow the "flash"—which often like a will-o'-the-wisp leads them astray—but they are not intelligent in their spiritual vision. They do not know that God is able, not only to deliver the mind from the enemy's grip but also to *renew it*, so that it becomes as clear as crystal, with "every rebellious thought brought into captivity."

We have seen that one reason why the liberation of the mind is so important is that it is the vehicle of the spirit. Has it never struck you how extraordinary it is that the children of God can hear so much and yet *express* so little? If you should ask one and another to intelligently transmit something of what they have heard, they cannot do it. They have listened to volumes of truth for years, and yet they have no power to transmit it and help a soul in need. And many of these hearers will tell you that they have received a baptism of the Spirit! The reason for this lies in the *unrenewed mind*. They may truly have received the Holy Spirit, but speaking reverently, He is "locked up" in their spirit, and cannot get through the blocked channel of the mind. One reason is that many children of God do not soak themselves, so to speak, in God's thoughts. They think that to read a text in the morning is enough, and so they do not get their mind fully renewed. All the working of the old mind is enmity against God, and that is why you find people prejudiced over truth. Whenever you find a man *prejudiced* over some truth he does not understand, it always means that there is some activity of the old mind. The mind is like a seed plot. We do not realize what we are taking in, or sowing in the ground for future use. If you only make a remark about some person you have sown a seed, and if it is a critical thought it is there ready to blaze into a "prejudice" at the first opportunity.

All this is so true that it is easy to see now why the apostle describes the "mind" as a stronghold which has to be taken for Christ, and brought into subjection to Him. It may not have occurred to us that much which we have looked upon as "natural" disability in the use of our minds is to some extent the work of the enemy, who pours into that mind, which has never been fully taken out of his power, his own visions, thoughts, ideas and ways.

7. The need of the mind to be fully renewed.

Now the question is, how can the mind become *fully* renewed, for if we are children of God, by the very entry of the truth of God there has been a *partial* renewal. Conversion itself is described in the Bible as, in the first instance, a "*change of mind.*" This is the meaning of the word "repent." The lexicon says the Latin word has the thought "to recover one's senses" and come to "a right understanding." So repentance means basically a "change of mind," to be accompanied by a change of heart.

8. The cross the place of deliverance.

But for full renewal of the mind we have to go to the cross, and learn its message that "our old man was crucified with Christ." This is inclusive of the old carnal, darkened, fleshly mind. This comes out clearly in the words of Ephesians 4:22–23, as following the apostle's description of the darkened and empty mind in verses 17 and 18. The "old man" crucified is here bidden to be "put off" by the believer, so that he may be *"renewed in the spirit of his mind."* The way of renewal, therefore, is via Calvary. The first need is the knowledge of the state of mind by nature, and that a "change of mind" at conversion does not go deep enough to fully deliver the soul from the power of the enemy in one's thought life and mental activities. Then there must be a deliberate and definite "putting off" of the "old man" in the aspect of the old carnal mind, for the bringing captive to Christ of every thought. What is wanted, then, is to recognize that *the unrenewed mind is part of the old creation* that has to be put off at the cross. Remember that God does just what you trust Him to do. We need to realize that what God wants is even a "cold-blooded" act of faith as the believer says, "I *trust* Thee to do this." We would like Him to do the whole work at once, but He has planned that we depend upon Him step by step for everything.

Some of you have come to understand your position of being crucified with Christ upon the cross. The Holy Spirit will now take you into the *details* of all that this means. He may throw light on the "circumference" to show where the old life is lodged, so that it may be dealt with. When Christ is your life, Christ is enthroned at the center. That new Center life (*Christ* at the center) has to be worked out as you perpetually hold the position "I am crucified." Then the Holy Spirit will throw light upon every part of the circumference that is as yet undealt with. Today we are dealing with the mind. Here you need to say, "Lord,

I trust Thee to give me a renewed mind, and I agree to part with the old one." When someone speaks to you about another in a manner likely to cause a bias in your mind, you will then readily say, "Please don't. I have not met the person. I should like to meet him without any preconceived ideas about him." But supposing today you have handed this old man to the cross and are trusting God to give you a new one, *do you think the enemy will give up his ground without a fight?* Do you think that every "rebellious thought" is going to be brought into subjection easily? This brings us to our next observation.

9. *The mind and its practical liberation.*

We must recognize that the mind *continues* to be the strategic battleground, even when we have claimed the deliverance of Calvary. We must know how the liberation of the mind has to be actually worked out, and for this the Spirit of God needs our active cooperation. The believer needs to recognize that the attacks of the emissaries of Satan are *primarily directed at the mind.* Notice how Paul realizes this, and describes the mind of the Christian as the strategic battleground for the enemy.

"I fear," he writes to the Corinthians, "lest by any means . . . your *minds should be corrupted . . .*" and then he tells them how this would come about. "If he that cometh preacheth another Jesus . . . or if ye receive another spirit . . . or another gospel" (2 Cor. 11:3–4). So the danger of the Christian is false teaching getting into the *mind*, and diverting him from the simple gospel of Christ. It is to this end that Satan transforms himself into an angel of light. How few realize that Satan can give spurious light to the mind, even light about a "Jesus" who is not the Lord, and minister "another spirit" which is not the Holy Spirit, and through his instruments preach a "gospel" which is not the gospel of the grace of God.

The danger which the apostle wrote about to the Corinthians is increased today a thousandfold because of the psychic forces that are at work in the world—because, too, of the tremendous emphasis upon and development of the mental life at the present time, and because the enemy is actively at work seeking to break down the mental powers of God's children through the strain of the conflict of life. There are grave dangers all about us from counterfeit guidance, counterfeit visions and counterfeit plans, all coming from *the enemy's work upon the mind.* Never was there a time when believers so needed the "helmet of salvation" to cover their heads from the foe. The air is full of suggestions by "the prince of the power of the air," flashing thoughts and ideas into the minds of men. Take what is called the "higher criticism." Picture a man who is without the knowledge of the new birth through the cross of Christ, reading in his study. Wonderful "thoughts" which come into his mind are given out as the result of his own thinking, and the world marvels at the "brilliance" of this scholar. Alas, the "brilliance" of a mind which the Word of God declares is *blinded by the god of this age*, and energized by "the spirit which now worketh in the children of disobedience," *is really darkness in the sight of God*. What the unrenewed mind is capable of producing under the energizing of the spirits of Satan can be seen for example in the textbook of Christian Science, where words seem to be spun out as a spider spins his web, as empty as the gossamer threads composing it.

The dangerous output of "great minds" thus wrought upon by the prince of the power of the air will increase as the dispensation hastens to its close, and the children of God will be caught in the meshes of these "fantasies" unless they have their own minds renewed and kept sober by the truth of God. They need in the face of these dangers to guard against overwork which may bring about overstrain of the mind, making them incapable of sober judgment.

10. The practical way of victory.

How is the mind of the child of God to be actually set free from the enemy's control and renewed by the Spirit of God? We have seen that there is deliverance *via Calvary,* but there is also a practical line of action on the part of the believer. The first question to be faced is one concerning control. There may be a wrong thought about this which must not be overlooked. You are quite aware that your mind is out of control, and you have been praying that God would "control" it independently of you. But all in vain. Some times your mind is full of wandering thoughts and your imagination is inflamed, or it is heavy, passive or sluggish, and unusable. *It is practically out of your control, and is uncontrolled by God.* What is the reason? You may never have taken your mind out of control of the enemy (see 2 Cor. 4:4) and deliberately handed it over to the death of the cross, and trusted God to give you a new mind. Numbers of God's people know that their minds are neither under God's control nor their own. And it is often because the enemy has put a thought in their minds which has laid hold of the mind until it is mastered by it. Whenever you find a person who can only talk of "one thing," it is best to shun them. It always reveals the fact that the mind of that one is not under control. If God is controlling your thoughts and mind, you can choose both what you think and when you will speak. But if you say, "If I don't speak what is in my mind at once I shall lose it," *then you had better "lose it."* How many pour upon you their "thinks" and never heed what effect it will have upon you. Oh how we all need some sober light upon the realm of the mind! Recently a letter came to me in which I was told of a Christian man who said, "My wife was a most beautiful Christian. But suddenly the thought was suggested in the middle of the night that she had committed the unpardonable sin, and now she is in a mental home and I can do nothing, and my little children are without their mother." The minister said to the poor man that it seemed to be of the enemy; so they knelt down and the minister asked that if Satan had shot this thing into the mind of the wife, the Lord would prove it to the husband through the victory of Calvary. Praise God, within a fortnight she was back in her home.

11. The new mind and its characteristics.

When the mind is renewed, the Spirit of God fulfills the promise of God, where He says, "I will put My laws into their hearts, and *in their minds will I write them*" (Heb. 10:16). Thus we obtain the "mind" of Christ (1 Cor. 2:16). What that "mind" is we read in Philippians 2:5-8. The practical life is changed only so far as we are "transformed" by the "renewing of the mind" (Rom. 12:2). Christ's "mind" was to obey God, even unto the death of the cross. That "mind" in us becomes an armor. "Arm yourselves likewise with the same mind" (1 Pet. 4:1), i.e., Christ's mind towards the cross. "*Christ suffered*," we say, and as our minds dwell upon His sufferings, and the Holy Spirit shows us the separation from sin which fellowship with Him brings about, we too choose to suffer, and we are "armed" by having His mind. Thus the new mind becomes "stayed upon God," instead of being tossed about by distracting thoughts. And a mind stayed on God means perfect peace (see Isa. 26:3).

12. The "new mind" as the vehicle of the Holy Spirit.

In Ephesians 1:18 we read, "The eyes of your understanding" being "filled with light." Here is the mind illumined by the Spirit. It is the vehicle of light. You *see* with the mind, you *feel* with the spirit. David said, "My *spirit* made diligent search." The mind is enlightened from God in the spirit, illuminating the mind. This brings into action the perceptive faculty of the mind, whereby the believer is able to spiritually discern spiritual things. The various marginal readings of 1 Corinthians 2:13 show the new mind in use. It is able to "discriminate," "examine," "combine," "compare" and "explain" spiritual things which the "natural" man knows nothing about. The perceptive faculty of the mind renewed by the Spirit of God enables us more clearly to know how to prove the good and acceptable will of God. "If any man walk in the day, he stumbleth not," said the Lord (John 11:9). In broad daylight a man does not need to fall over stones in his path before he sees them. And so it is spiritually. With a new mind filled with light by the Spirit, the believer sees the path wherein he should walk, and discerns the will of God clearly without the confusion and perplexities of the partially renewed mind.

13. *The guarding of the new mind.*

There is no part of the renewed believer which does not require guarding. This is especially true of the mind which has been renewed. First there is a "girding up" of "the loins of the mind" (see 1 Pet. 1:13), which is necessary. This means that you must never let the mind become "slack," or careless in its thinking, or it will soon fall a prey to the watching enemy. The mind should never be idle, or without "grist for the mill!" It must be active if it is in a normal condition. The apostle also bids the believer see that he does not admit an "anxious" thought (see Phil. 4:6), but at once to transmit any that come, to God. If he does this, the "peace of God" will garrison his mind, and keep it in peace. But he must do more: *he must give the mind work to do*, and let it have true, honest, just, pure and lovely things to "think" about (see see Phil. 4:8).

Then again, the believer with the new mind must "think soberly" (Rom. 12:3), especially about himself. He must avoid dwelling on "high things" (12:16), and in the path of soberness take no step which is not the outcome of deliberate judgment and decision. Every "thought" led captive (2 Cor. 10:5) means the deliberate weighing of every word and action in the light of God. Thus we shall be able to walk with God in these days of peril, and be sober when others are carried away by the spurious workings of the enemy. Do not follow or trust what we may describe as "flashes" of light to the mind, because the Holy Spirit in your spirit works out into the mind His light in calm, intelligent, deliberate illumination from within. Because of the dangers today *we cannot trust anything that comes from without.* It is not that these "flashes" are necessarily wrong, but that you cannot trust them. Neither can anything said on the impulse of the moment be trusted. Supposing a thought comes, it should be turned over and over and pondered over in the presence of God. "Am I to take this thought as from Thee? If so, please bring it back to me again and again, and show me." Thus you will learn to walk carefully and accurately in the will of God. We need to be encased in the armor of Christ. God dwelling in our spirit—pouring the light into our mind, according to His written Word—will enable us to carefully and prayerfully walk with Him.

THE VITAL SERIES

The Battle for the Mind .... Jessie Penn-Lewis
Catching Men .... Watchman Nee
Challenge .... Roy Hession
Life in the Blood .... Andrew Murray
The Life That Wins .... Charles G. Trumbull
Practical Holiness .... Evan H. Hopkins
**A Synopsis of
    The Normal Christian Life** ...... Watchman Nee
**Trusting the Spirit: Selections from
    The Spirit of Christ** .... Andrew Murray
Why This Waste? .... Watchman Nee
Yield Yourself to God .... Andrew Murray

These other titles from our Vital Series are also available from your Christian bookstore or from:

CLC • Publications
P.O. Box 1449, Fort Washington, PA 19034

Fax: (215) 542-7580 **E-mail:** orders@clcpublications.com